To Katie and Cal...
My first siblings and the inspiration for
this book and those that will follow.

My Brother's Sister

Written by: Ashley Coates

Illustrated by: Amy Carroll

A book for siblings impacted by Autism
Book One of the Super Siblingz Series

Layout & Design by Sonya Tanae Fort of S. Tanae Designs: www.stanaedesigns.com

Dear Super Siblingz,

Thank you for reading our book! We know that sometimes having a brother or sister with special needs can be pretty tough. Lots of siblings sometimes feel angry, annoyed or frustrated. But, they also love their sibling and have fun playing games, going places together and just hanging out with them. We hope our book helps you to remember how super you are and how lucky your sibling is to have you as a brother or sister!

Your friend,

Ashley

I have a brother
who does some odd things...

He spins and he rocks,
flaps his arms like they're wings.

He hides when it's noisy,
        covers his ears if it's loud...

But when others are silent,
he sure draws a crowd.

He doesn't like buttons,
zippers or tags...

He wants sweat pants and soft
clothes in his shopping bags.

My Mom says that's Sensory,
whatever that means...

I think it's silly,
just put on some jeans!

No parks or pools,
and forget the beach...

He has to stay within
my Dad's arms reach.

Those places are not safe
for a brother like mine...

"Let's go," they say,
maybe some other time.

I guess I'll play inside,
Or stay in the yard...

Being his sister
sure can be hard!

Other kids go on
vacations and trips...

To far away places
on planes or in ships.

We go to therapies,
doctors and clinics...

I'm bored and would
rather be having a picnic!

My Brother's not all bad,
he's funny and smart!

He plays the piano
and loves music and art.

He can't use his voice,
like my friends or me...

He talks with his iPad,
the fancy word is
Assistive Technology!

We like to watch movies
and play on the swings,

we're kind of different
but like the same things!

I may take vitamins,
while he takes his pills...

But, we both pour syrup
down tall pancake hills!

My Brother has Autism,
and that's hard at times...

But I wouldn't trade him,
I'm glad that he's mine!

Glossary

Sometimes the words people use when they talk about your brother or sister are tricky to understand! This might help you to learn what these words mean.

Autism: (Aw-tih-zum) Every day, our brains try to understand all of the things that we see, smell, hear, taste and touch. But when someone's brain has trouble interpreting these things, it can make it hard to talk, listen, understand, play, and learn.

Sensory: (Sens-o-ree) We use our senses to hear, taste and touch. Kids who have sensory issues often feel things much more strongly. They can be annoyed or irritated by things that we might not notice, like a tag on their shirt or a loud noise.

Assistive Technology: (Assis-tiv-tek-nol-o-jee) Assistive technology is a piece of equipment used to help kids communicate (talk) with their friends and family when their voices don't work normally or they have a hard time finding the right words. Some kids use a computer or a picture book to help others know what they want to say.

Dear Super Parents,

Thank you for finding our book and sharing it with your child. We've learned that siblings have the longest relationship with their brother or sister with special needs, and in some instances, they will become the caregiver and decision maker when you no longer can. We hope that with our book, your child will find comfort in knowing that they are not alone in their frustrations or the joys that come from having a special sibling. We encourage you to read this book with your child and use it as a tool for discussing how they feel about their brother or sister.

Having worked with siblings, and having heard their unfiltered, honest feedback we know that they sometimes feel less important because of their lack of a special need.

They also tend to feel pressure to be the perfect child, in an effort to not add to your parental stress.

We applaud the commitment you make each and every day to all of your children and encourage you to take a deep breath and pat yourself on the back.

For additional information, or to ask a question, please visit the sibling page on www.CoatesCorner.com. You can also visit www.siblingsupport.org to find a Sibshop in your area and learn more about the sibling experience.

All my best,

Ashley

Ashley

Amy Carrol, llustrator

 Amy Carroll is an office manager by day, and illustrator extraordinaire by night. Her passions include cupcake decorating, reading, watching Disney movies and coloring (of course)! During the summer, Amy spends her time developing a Theater Camp for children, 6 years and counting!

Ashley Coates, Author

 Ashley Coates is a first time author, but long time supporter of children and families impacted by disability. When she isn't trying to find a word that rhymes with "sensory", she loves to spend time with her family and friends, take naps with her dog LuLu and shop for shoes. Ashley works with the Federation for Children with Special Needs, The Massachusetts Down Syndrome Congress and is a Fellow in the LEND program at the Institute for Community Inclusion at Children's Hospital Boston.